Simple Strategies That Work!

Helpful Hints for All Educators of Students with Autism and Related Disabilities

Brenda Smith Myles
Diane Adreon
Dena Gitlitz

FUTURE HORIZONS

www.fhautism.com
info@fhautism.com
817.277.0727

Simple strategies that work! : helpful hints for all educators of students with Asperger syndrome, high-functioning autism, and related disabilities / Brenda Smith Myles, Diane Adreon, Dena Gitlitz. – 1st ed. 2006.

p. ; cm.

ISBN-13: 978-1-931282-99-4
ISBN-10: 1-931282-99-4
LCCN: 2006927642
Includes bibliographical references.

1. Autistic children – Education. 2. Asperger's syndrome – Patients – Education. 3. Teachers of children with disabilities – Handbooks, manuals, etc. 4. Teaching – Aids and devices.
I. Adreon, Diane. II. Gitlitz, Dena. III. Title.
LC4717 .M95 2006
371.94–dc22   0606

Simple Strategies That Work!

TABLE OF CONTENTS

INTRODUCTION

Children and youth with Asperger Syndrome (AS), high-functioning autism (HFA), pervasive developmental disorders-not otherwise specified (PDD-NOS),[1] and related exceptionalities have great potential, but all too often their abilities are not realized. In part this is because their skills mask their difficulties. That is, many students with HFA/AS have impressive knowledge on particular subjects and an exceptional rote memory. These attributes tend to cloud the fact that they do not understand aspects of the school environment that other students pick up automatically without direct instruction. Often referred to as the "hidden curriculum," this includes such otherwise generally understood "rules" as "When having to go to the restroom at school, quietly tell the teacher or another adult instead of announcing it to the whole class."

In addition, most students with AS/HFA have poor organizational skills, and handwriting is laborious and difficult for them. They often want to make friends but don't know how. Besides, students with AS/HFA often have sensory integration issues that can make them extra sensitive to light, sounds, tastes, smells, etc.

AS/HFA encompasses a complex range of difficulties and challenges, and how they are manifested in a particular student is only part of the solution to helping students succeed. Definitive steps must be taken to implement interventions that match their individual needs and empower them to be successful.

---

[1] For ease of reading the term AS/HFA will be used to describe these students.

Table 1

CHARACTERISTICS OF STUDENTS WITH AS/HFA

- Impairments in social understanding & social skills

- Sensory issues (personal space, sounds/noises, movement, tactile, taste, smell, light, temperature)

- Often interact more successfully with adults or younger children than same-aged peers

- Difficulty establishing and maintaining friendships with peers

- Difficulty understanding and using body language (i.e., eye gaze, gestures, and facial expression)

- Expressive skills often mask comprehension problems

- May "parrot" back information without comprehending the content

- Often fail to seek clarification

- Interpret language literally

- Difficulty in understanding & discussing feelings

- Often show limited interest in others

- Strong preference for sameness

- Excessive time & energy devoted to special interests

- Attention challenges

- Poor organizational skills

- Difficulty regulating their emotions

- Poor handwriting

- Impaired gross-motor skills

ABOUT THIS BOOK

The following strategies can help a student with AS/HFA on the road to success. The strategies can be applied to students of all ages – preschool through high school. In addition, they can be applied in all settings – in the classroom, on the playground, in the hallways at school, during lunch, physical education, recess, and specials, as well as on field trips.

Besides, the strategies, while effective, are simple enough for everyone to use. That is, in addition to teachers and related support personnel, administrators, office staff, cafeteria workers, bus drivers, and paraprofessionals will find that these supports lay the groundwork for more successful experiences for students with AS/HFA. In many cases, these strategies are helpful for all students, but for the student with AS/HFA, they are essential.

Simple Strategies That Work

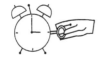 **1.** Operate on Asperger Time

 2. Manage the Environment

 3. Create a Balanced Agenda That Conserves Energy

 **4.** Share the Agenda

 5. Simplify Language

 6. Set a Calm, Positive Tone

 7. Live Out Loud

 8. Be Generous With Praise

 9. Listen to the Words

 **10.** Provide Reassurance

1. OPERATE ON ASPERGER TIME

Children and youth with AS/HFA have an internal clock that differs from that of most of their same-age peers. Asperger time means, "Twice as much time, half as much done." That is, students with AS/HFA often need additional time to complete assignments, to gather materials, and to orient themselves during transitions.

Make sure that the student has ample time to complete organizational and related tasks, such as

- taking out and organizing books, paper, and pencil on her desk
- putting away materials
- finding and turning in homework
- moving from classroom to classroom
- organizing her backpack
- eating lunch
- dressing out in physical education
- organizing materials to go home after school

Modify Requirements

Also, modify requirements so they match the student's pace. Table 2 provides sample modifications that allow a child with AS/HFA to operate successfully on Asperger time.

Reduce or Eliminate Handwriting

Another modification that supports the child is to remove extensive handwriting requirements from assignments and other tasks. Most children and youth with AS/HFA have handwriting problems and, as a result, they cannot do their best work when having to write. In order to operate on Asperger time, allow the child to dictate or use a keyboard, for example, instead of writing in long hand.

Table 2

SAMPLE MODIFICATIONS TO HELP STUDENTS WHO OPERATE ON ASPERGER TIME

• Reduce the number of problems on a page by (a) circling the problems that the child has to complete or (b) masking the problems the child does not need to complete	• Have the student use a personal digital assistant or pocket computer instead of a handwritten planner
• Change short-answer questions to true/false or multiple-choice questions	• Have the child dictate book reports and similar assignments into a tape recorder instead of having to write by hand
• Allow the child to dictate answers into a tape recorder	• Have another child write for the child with AS/HFA
• Allow the child use a computer for written assignments instead of having to write them by hand	• Use a time timer (www.timetimer.com) to allow the child to see time passing visually
• Provide a five-, four-, three-, two-, one-minute transition reminder	• Provide early or late release for passing periods

Avoid Rushing

When time constraints are added to an already stressful day, the student with AS/HFA can become overwhelmed and even immobilized. He may freeze or begin to have a tantrum, rage, or meltdown.

Regardless of the student's outward behavior – whether he withdraws or engages in explosive behavior – he cannot comprehend what is being said to him or follow directions when rushed. That is, he is no longer in a learning mode. Thus, failure to operate on Asperger time can seriously limit the time the student has available for learning, changing the original definition of Asperger time to: "Twice as much time, half as much done *unless you are in a hurry*, then multiply by 10."

2.
MANAGE THE ENVIRONMENT

Children and youth with AS/HFA often do not have the organizational and planning skills that help them navigate through their day successfully. They don't inherently understand routines, how to handle changes in their environment, or predict what can happen next. This inability or difficulty in managing the environment causes stress and anxiety, which results in lower academic and social performance, decreased attention to task, and potential increases in behavior problems.

To help them manage, establish and teach students routines for all activities that occur consistently in school. For example, the student needs to know when and how he can sharpen his pencil, where to turn in homework, how his books should be arranged in a desk or locker, what books should be taken to which class, when to go to his locker, etc.

Table 3 lists potential routines that should be taught directly to students with AS/HFA. Some students have benefited from having a small booklet or list that explains the routines. Further, if this information is posted in the class and directly taught to students, *everyone* will benefit, not just the child with AS/HFA.

The following is an example of a simple routine for pencil sharpening. Its explicitness prevents uncertainty and countless questions.

PENCIL SHARPENING ROUTINE

It is always good to have more than one pencil sharpened. Use this routine if you have a pencil that you can write with until you can go to a pencil sharpener:

1. Wait until students are quietly working independently or in small groups or until there is a break between classes or activities.

2. Bring your pencils to the pencil sharpener. If you have two pencils to be sharpened, bring them both.

3. Without talking to your neighbor, sharpen each pencil.

4. Quietly return to your desk. If you do not have a working pencil and need one immediately, always request permission to sharpen your pencil.

Table 3

ROUTINES THAT NEED TO BE DIRECTLY TAUGHT TO CHILDREN AND YOUTH WITH AS/HFA

- How to ask for help

- How and when to sharpen pencils

- When and what to throw away and where

- How to ask to go to the bathroom

- How to obtain school supplies when they forget to bring them to class

- How and when to hand in homework

- How to pass out papers

- How to organize materials on their desk

- How to place school supplies in a locker, backpack or desk so that they are easily accessible

- How to make up missed work due to absences or related reasons

- How to line up for lunch, recess, etc.

- How to walk down the hall in a line with other students

- How to get ready to transition to another activity within the same class

- How to get ready to transition to another activity that is not within the same class

- How to get ready for recess

- How to get ready to go home

- What to do during free time

- How to navigate lunchtime

Prepare for Change

The student with AS/HFA has to continually sort through, process, and integrate what he is to do each day even if there are no schedule changes. Therefore, any changes, and in particular unexpected changes, no matter how small they may seem to others, can increase anxiety. Whenever possible, provide consistency in the schedule and avoid sudden changes.

Prepare the child for the change by discussing it in advance, overviewing a social narrative, such as a Social Story™ (created by Carol Gray; Gray, 2000), on the change, or showing a picture of the change. For example, it is unwise to rearrange classroom furniture or change seating assignments without introducing it ahead of time to the child with AS/HFA. The introduction may include reviewing a picture of what the rearranged classroom will look like.

A visual schedule that incorporates the student's activities is also helpful. At the bottom of the schedule, an icon with the words "Sometimes the Schedule Changes" appears (Figure 1). This may be used to introduce specific changes. In addition, remind the student daily that changes can occur and that they can be managed. This may be done by using a change in routine card as illustrated in Figure 2.

Figure 1
DAILY SCHEDULE

Today is Monday, May 22, 2006

Attendance		8:15
Math	8:20	– 9:00
Reading and Centers	9:00	– 10:00
Spelling	10:00	– 10:15
Writing	10:15	– 10:45
Assembly	10:45	– 11:30
Lunch & Recess	11:30	– 12:15
Music	12:30	– 1:15
Science	1:15	– 1:50
Read Aloud	1:50	– 2:20
Journal	2:10	– 2:25
Get Ready to Go		2:25
Bell Rings		2:30

SOMETIMES THE SCHEDULE CHANGES

Figure 2
CHANGE IN ROUTINE CARD

NOTICE: _____ will be changed on _____

because _____

_____

The new _____

is _____

When planning activities, make the student aware that the activities are *planned*, not guaranteed. That is, emphasize that activities can be changed, cancelled, or rescheduled. In addition, create and share backup plans. Kristi Sakai, author of *Finding Our Way* (2005), calls this "priming and predicting."

PRIMING IN ACTION

Ms. Hunter announced to her class, "Instead of math tomorrow, we are going to have an assembly featuring Bill Nye the Science Guy. He will do an experiment in the gymnasium on electricity. Be prepared for the light to go on and off and for loud sounds [*Priming*]. It will be an exciting assembly that most of us will look forward to! However, what if Bill Nye cancels the assembly? It is not likely that he will, but there is always a chance. If he cancels, we will stay in the class and do math [*Predicting*]. I have a special math activity planned just in case. Remember – our plan is to go to the assembly to see Bill Nye. Our backup plan is to stay in class and learn something new in math."

When an unavoidable situation occurs, be flexible and recognize that change is stressful and adapt expectations and your language accordingly. For example, a teacher could state, "Our class is scheduled to go to the park tomorrow. If it rains, you can read your favorite book on dinosaurs."

Incorporate the Student's Preferences

The environment may also be managed by incorporating student preferences. It is often useful to keep an "emergency kit" of favored items to increase the student's comfort level and, therefore, decrease her stress. (Find out ahead of time from the student, parents or other students what is soothing and comforting to the student.) Such a kit could include a drawing pad and markers, an educational handheld computer game, a book, or a favorite fidget. For example, when going on a field trip, the student might be assigned to sit with a group of preferred peers or be given a favorite toy or object to bring along. Or if the field trip will include lunch, the student can be given access to the menu the day before so he can plan what he wants to eat. That way he won't have to worry all day that he may not like what is being served.

The "emergency kit" is also handy for the times when there is "down time" in the schedule as students with AS/HFA often have difficulty knowing how to manage own behavior when they are waiting for the next activity. Waiting in line, waiting for others to finish eating, and waiting for their turn can all be problems. The terms "wait" or "waiting" are almost always associated with "potential problems."

Build in Relaxation

Incorporating relaxation time into the schedule, especially when novel activities are introduced, is also extremely important. Students with AS/HFA need "time away" from the stressors of the classroom. Because these students have difficulty calming themselves when they become anxious, down time, removal to a safe place, home base, or cool zone can be effective ways to manage the environment.

TIME AWAY

A safe place, home base, or cool zone is an identified place within the classroom or another location within the school where the student can go to calm down and regroup. This is meant to be a positive intervention, in which the goal is for the student to eventually be able to recognize when he is overwhelmed and be able to remove himself from the situation, self-calm, and return — ready to work. This is not to be confused with time-out.

Strategies such as the incredible 5-Point Scale (Buron & Curtis, 2004) (see Figure 3) and simple relaxation techniques such as those presented in Figure 4 (Buron, 2004) can be helpful tools, along with home base, for teaching the student how to recognize and communicate the magnitude of his distress and learning ways to self-calm and possibly prevent his behavior from escalating.

Provide Choices

Finally, a simple way to manage the environment is to offer choices. The opportunity to make a choice provides the student more control, and when she feels in control of a situation, she is less likely to be anxious or upset. Choice making also increases attention, promotes independence, and reduces problem behaviors.

Figure 3

Name: _____ My Scale _____

Rating	Looks like	Feels like	I can try to
5			
4			
3			
2			
1			

Figure 4
MY CALMING SEQUENCE

This is when I need to fight back!
First, I can squeeze
my hands together.

Next, I can take three really slow,
deep breaths. Slow in – slow out,
slow in – slow out, slow in – slow out.

Then I can sit down, rub my legs and
close my eyes. Now I feel more
like a 3 or a 2.

I can think about happy things, like my
dog or my stuffed lion, or our family
cabin in the summer. Now I am at a 1.

3.
CREATE A BALANCED AGENDA THAT CONSERVES ENERGY

Think of students with AS/HFA as having a limited amount of energy available to them each day. Their energy "reserve" can vary from day to day. In addition, tasks, demands, and environments can make differing demands. For example, attending to a difficult task is more draining than is reading about a special interest. Similarly, unstructured times place more demands on the child than following a schedule. For example, waiting in a crowded gym or the lunchroom prior to school starting, movement in the hallways, lunchtime, and recess can be overwhelming for the student with AS/HFA. Crowded, noisy environments along with an agenda of non-preferred activities can be particularly difficult.

Even preferred activities can be draining as illustrated in the following scenario.

TOO MUCH OF A GOOD THING

John's teacher prepared him well for the morning class trip to the local museum's exhibit on ancient Egyptian artifacts, John's special interest, and an assembly featuring a magician in the afternoon.

For the museum trip, she gave him a list of exhibited items and a schedule of field-trip activities; besides, he had seen a video created by the museum. For the assembly, his teacher had prepared John by showing him where he would sit during the assembly and providing him with the magician's agenda. John voiced excitement over the assembly because a magician had performed at his birthday party the year before. The teacher anticipated that the day would be enjoyable for John because of his special interest in Egyptology.

The day began well; John followed the schedule and attended to the exhibit. However, when the class returned to school for the assembly, John appeared distracted and somewhat ill at ease. John's teacher overviewed the assembly agenda with the entire class, making sure she asked John questions to ensure that he understood the schedule. He transitioned into the assembly well, but 10 minutes into it, he slid to the floor, loudly proclaiming that the magician did not do the right tricks. His behavior continued to escalate until he was offered a fidget and a pass to go to his home base.

John's teacher was puzzled – she thought she had prepared him thoroughly for the day and therefore expected him to enjoy the activities. Normally, both activities would have been enjoyable for John, but not on the same day. The trip to the museum in the morning had used up John's energy reserve so he had nothing left in his system for the assembly and therefore became overwhelmed. These two activities, although each potentially enjoyable, were not pleasurable.

Monitor Demands

Given the limited energy reserve of students with AS/HFA, it is essential to monitor the demands of the daily schedule or certain classes or activities and restructure them, as needed. To do so, it is necessary to prioritize.

Ask, "What are the most important activities or tasks for the child to achieve?" and make modifications accordingly to ensure that major objectives are achieved. For example, a student with AS/HFA may need early release from class to walk to the next class through the hall when not crowded in order to better concentrate during the upcoming class – algebra. The energy the student would normally use to meet the sensory challenges of passing time (i.e., bumping into other students, rushing to get from locker to class on time, screening out noise) is "saved" for when it is needed – in this instance, for algebra.

If students are easily overwhelmed, balancing the agenda is particularly important. For example, free time may have to be structured with prescribed activities. "Free time," which is considered fun for neurotypical students, is often challenging for students with AS/HFA because of noise levels, lack of predictability, as well as social skills challenges. Therefore, it may be necessary to incorporate a balance of low-stress, high-pleasure activities within a demanding schedule.

Table 4
STRATEGIES FOR BALANCING THE AGENDA

- Engage the child in a familiar or calming activity early in the school day to prepare her for work.

- Incorporate special interests into assignments.

- Alternate difficult and less difficult tasks as well as interchange preferred and non-preferred activities.

- Provide "down time" in the schedule.

- Make occupational therapy-prescribed de-stressing, alerting, and calming activities available throughout the day. (A brief listing of potential activities is included in Table 5.)

Use Calming and Alerting Activities

It is important to request the services of an occupational therapist to assess the student's sensory issues and recommend a sensory diet. A well-planned sensory diet can help the student maintain his behavior and assist in regulating his arousal level throughout the day.

Table 5 provides examples of the types of sensory activities that can assist in calming the student who is over-aroused or raising the arousal level if necessary.

Table 5

CALMING AND ALERTING SENSORY ACTIVITIES

Sensory Area	Calming Activities	Alerting Activities
Tactile	• Wear weighted vests or ankle weights • Snuggle under blankets • Play with resistive putty	• Sustain light touch to the palm of the hand • Hold something cold • Gently and quickly rub the skin • Take a cool shower or wash face with cool washcloth • Receive a light back scratch • Pet a dog or cat • Handle fidget items
Proprioceptive	• Push heavy furniture • Push a heavy cart to deliver library books or retrieve lunch trays • Carry boxes, laundry basket, or unload groceries • Vacuum the floor • Do "wheelbarrow walk" • Carry a weighted blanket • Wear a fanny pack • Carry a weighted backpack • Jump into a squishy pile of pillows	• Help by passing out papers, erasing the board, or delivering a message • Exercise, dance, wriggle
Vestibular	• Jump on a trampoline or do jumping jacks • Swing on playground equipment • Rock in a rocking chair • Roll back and forth in a barrel • Take a break to do an errand • Swing in a hammock	• Jump on a trampoline or do jumping jacks • Hang upside down on a jungle gym • Ride a scooter down a ramp • Sit and bounce on a therapy ball • Stand and twirl in a circle • Bend over and place head between legs • Do somersaults and cartwheels
Gustatory	• Chew or suck on mild flavors such as suckers, hard candy, or chew toys • Suck thick liquids through a straw • Drink from a sports water bottle • Chew/suck on a keychain or necklace • Chew/suck on a pen top • Play a musical instrument • Blow whistles, bubbles, feathers, balloons, cotton balls, etc. • Drink warm liquids, such as hot chocolate, cider, soup • Engage in eating chewing, sucking, and blowing activities • Engage in blowing activities paired with eye-tracking exercises (blow ping-pong ball with straw)	• Eat crunchy foods, such as pretzels, ice, carrots, celery, apples • Eat chewy foods, such as licorice, taffy, beef jerky, gum • Blow whistles, bubbles, feathers, balloons, cotton balls, etc. • Eat ice or popsicles • Keep a water bottle with cold water on desk • Eat crunchy, sour, chewy, salty, or cold foods • Engage in eating chewing, sucking and blowing activities

Sensory Area	Calming Activities	Alerting Activities
Olfactory	• Burn a vanilla scented candle (if child, under adult supervision) • Smell potpourri in the classroom • Incorporate preferred scents within academic tasks (e.g., writing with a scented pen) • Use scented crayons or markers	• Use scented lotion or soap between activities • Spray a citrus room deodorizer before academic activities • Use scented materials in projects • Receive scratch-and-sniff stickers as a reward
Auditory	• Listen to quiet music with slow, even beat • Listen to soft singing or humming • Cover ears when a loud or unexpected noise happens • Work in a quiet environment • Use headphones to shield from noise	• Listen to music with varied pitch, sound loudness or uneven/fast beat • Speak with animated high and low voice • Enjoy frequent opportunities to examine novel sound-producing toys (e.g., chimes, squeeze toys, rain stick) • Use sound-producing materials to complete classroom projects (e.g., talking calculator books on tape, Yak Back [Yes! Entertainment Corp.; 1-925-847-9444] for verbal directions) • Prepare in advance for loud/strange noises
Visual	• Work in dim light or with lights turned off • Block distractions by using a screen, room divider, or study carrel • Wear sunglasses • Provide visual materials such as a glitter wand, oil and water toys, fish tank • Work at distraction-free desk • Work in soft or limited light and pastel colors • Work in natural rather than artificial light	• Work in bright lights • Use a flashlight to point or highlight important information • Use brightly colored paper • Use a highlighter to underline important text • Use colored chalk • Use a slant board to place materials at an angle • Use bright lights or colors

Adapted with permission from *Learn to Move, Move to Learn! Sensorimotor Early Childhood Activity Themes* by Jenny Clark Brack, 2004; Shawnee Mission, KS: Autism Asperger Publishing Company; and *Sensation Station* by Lisa Robbins and Nancy Miller, 2006. Shawnee Mission, KS: Autism Asperger Publishing Company.

PLEASE NOTE: These activities should *not* be incorporated into a student's schedule without consulting an occupational therapist who is well versed in sensory integration.

4.
SHARE THE AGENDA

While many children can quickly grasp and follow the daily schedule without being told and can readily adapt to changes, this is not the case for most students with AS/HFA. Unless they are directly told what will happen next, they cannot predict. Without seeing a visual schedule, they don't know the daily routine. In and of itself, this would not be problematic if students with AS/HFA were comfortable with "going with the flow" or participating in unplanned activities. But they are not! Activities that seem unpredictable easily cause anxiety, which can lead to problem behavior and lower performance.

Use Visual Supports

To help students cope, visual supports have proven very effective. These can be lists of activities to complete, books to take to class, and reminders of what to discuss with peers at lunch. Table 6 provides a list of visual supports that can be helpful to students with AS/HFA during their middle and high school years.

Sharing the agenda is also important because students with AS/HFA have difficulty distinguishing between essential and nonessential information. In addition, they often do not know things that many of us have learned incidentally or consider common sense. Thus, it is important to state the obvious.

For example, saying what you are doing helps the student accurately put together *what* you are doing with the *why* and the *how* as illustrated in the following example. Teacher: "While you're working on your essays I'm going to be at the back of the room, putting some of your best writing examples on the bulletin board. If you have a question, you can come to the back of the room to ask me, or raise your hand and I'll come over to you."

Table 6
VISUAL SUPPORTS FOR MIDDLE AND HIGH SCHOOL STUDENTS WITH AS/HFA

Type of Support	Purpose	Location	Brief Description
Map of school outlining classes	• To assist the student in navigating school halls	• Taped or velcroed™ inside locker • Velcroed inside back cover of textbook or folder/notebook	To help orient and structure the student. This map shows the student where her classes are, the order in which they take place and times to visit her locker.
List of classes, room numbers, books and other supplies needed	• To aid the student in getting to class with needed materials	• Taped or velcroed inside locker • Velcroed inside back cover of textbook or folder/notebook	This list works well with students who have difficulty with maps. It lists the class, room number, supplies needed and when to go to the class.
List of teacher expectations and routines for each class	• To help the student understand the environment	• Velcroed inside front cover of textbook or folder/notebook • Placed on a key ring that is kept in pocket or on backpack	To reduce anxiety associated with routines and lack thereof, this visual support details the routine that is to be followed in the classroom (such as what the student is to do upon entering class and when and where to turn in homework, what the student is to do upon entering class, etc.) and outlines particular characteristics that can help the student get along in class (such as Mrs. Johnson does not permit talking with neighbors and likes both feet on the floor at all times; Mr. Thomas allows students to bring a bottle of water to class).
Schedule of activities within the class	• To prepare the student for upcoming activities as well as assist in transitioning between activities	• Listed on the chalkboard or whiteboard	This list simply details what activities will occur during a given class. As each activity is completed, it can be erased, crossed out, or checked off.

Table 6

VISUAL SUPPORTS FOR MIDDLE AND HIGH SCHOOL STUDENTS WITH AS/HFA (CONT.)

Type of Support	Purpose	Location	Brief Description
Outlines and notes from lectures	• To facilitate the student's understanding of content material	• Prepared by teacher in advance and placed on student's desk • Notes taken by peer during class using carbon paper or photocopied and handed out at the end of class • Tape recording of lecture with tape recorder placed near teacher and tape discreetly provided to the student at the end of class	Many students with AS/HFA have fine-motor challenges that make it difficult for them to take notes. Others cannot take notes and listen at the same time. These supports alleviate these challenges and allow the student to focus on understanding the content.
Sample models of assignments	• To help the student understand exactly what is required	• Prepared in advance by the teacher and given to the student discreetly. This can be a copy of an actual assignment that received an "A" grade	A model of assignments helps students be visually aware of format requirements. They can then concentrate on the content.
List of test reminders	• To ensure that the student knows when a test occurs and what material will be covered	• Prepared in advance by the teacher and given to the student to allow sufficient time to study • Final reminder given the day before the test. Often presented on a colorful piece of paper and placed in the student's folder • A schoolwide homework hotline is helpful. If this is not available, a peer can serve as the homework hotline	A study guide that lists content and textbook pages covered in the test is helpful. This guide should include a timeline for studying and outline content to be studied each night and the approximate time required to do so. The teacher assumes responsibility for developing it, but then works with the student to complete the task independently.

Table 6

Visual Supports for Middle and High School Students With AS/HFA (cont.)

Type of Support	Purpose	Location	Brief Description
List of schedule changes	• To ensure that the student is prepared for change	• Written on the chalkboard or whiteboard • Prepared in advance by the teacher (at least one day prior to activity) and given to the student to place in notebook. If the activity is one that the student is not familiar with, the list should also include his behavioral responsibilities	This prompt helps students prepare for a change in routine. Including the responsibilities of the student in the activity helps her complete the activity with minimal stress/anxiety.
List of homework assignments	• To assist the student in understanding requirements so that he can complete homework independently	• Prepared in advance and given to the student discreetly. This homework support should include all relevant information such as due date, items to complete, format, etc.	Students with AS/HFA need written details of homework. Teachers often write on the board or the overhead the basic elements of homework and supplement them verbally as students write down the assignment. This is not sufficient for students with AS/HFA.
Cue to go to home base	• To prompt the student to leave class to lower her stress/anxiety level	• A small card, approximately the size of a business card, is carried by the teacher, who discreetly places it on the student's desk when home base is needed	Students with AS/HFA often do not recognize that they are entering the cycle for a tantrum, rage, or meltdown. When the teacher recognizes the behaviors associated with the start of the cycle, she can use this card to prompt the student to leave the room.

5.
SIMPLIFY LANGUAGE

Students with AS/HFA have significant social-communication problems, but it is often easy to forget about this aspect of the disability because the students are usually very verbal. Social-communication problems refer to the effective use and understanding of communication in a social context, including nonverbal communication such as eye gaze, facial expressions, body language, gestures, and tone of voice.

Many individuals with AS/HFA know words that others do not and have the uncanny ability to use them correctly in sentences, making us believe that they understand what they are talking about. In addition, they often answer questions by relying on rote memory without truly comprehending the answer. For example, queries from teachers, such as "Do you know what you are supposed to do?," frequently prompt an affirmative response even if the child does not know what to do, as illustrated in the following example.

COMPREHENSION NOT GUARANTEED

When Mrs. Little, a seventh-grade teacher, asked her class, "What was one of the most unpopular taxes passed by the British Government in 1765?," Shivang, a youth with AS/HFA, raised his hand to respond. "The Stamp Act was one of the most unpopular taxes ever passed by the British Government. It made a good deal of money from a series of seemingly insignificant 'stamps'."

Mrs. Little was very impressed with Shivang's comprehensive response. Unfortunately, his answer was a direct quote from his social studies book and represented no understanding of the Stamp Act; it only demonstrated his good rote memory. Not surprisingly, Mrs. Little was surprised when Shivang was unable to answer a similar essay question on the test.

Watch for Literalness

Many students with AS/HFA have difficulty understanding metaphors, idioms and sarcasm, or knowing what is meant when only nonverbal communication such as facial expressions or gestures is used. Further, these students don't understand generalities. For example, when Susan's mother asked Susan if she had science homework Monday and Tuesday night, Susan said no even though she had a science test on Thursday. From a literal standpoint, Susan would not have homework in science until Wednesday night – the night before the test. Unfortunately, responses like this are often misinterpreted as being noncompliant. Therefore, it is important to probe for understanding and comprehension.

When clarifying language, specificity is important – "Say what you mean and mean what you say." General instructions, such as "Clean out your desk," may not be specific enough for a student. He might interpret it as sharpening pencils and pushing all the books inside his desk while his teacher had in mind a very different sort of cleaning.

Many students with AS/HFA have characteristics similar to those of individuals with attention deficit hyperactivity disorder (ADHD). As a result, they have particular difficulty attending to group directions. The following clarifying strategies may help students attend to lectures and follow directions.

Table 7

STRATEGIES TO HELP STUDENTS ATTEND TO LECTURES AND FOLLOW DIRECTIONS

- Use the student's name prior to giving a direction or asking a question.
- Tap gently on the student's desk prior to giving a direction.
- Provide the student with questions in advance.
- Combine verbal instructions with pictures, gestures, demonstrations, and written instructions.
- Have the student demonstrate that she understands or paraphrase what she is to do. Do not rely on yes/no responses to indicate comprehension.

Be specific when providing instructions to ensure that the student knows *what to do, how to do it,* and *when to do it.* Be clear and clarify as needed. This includes keeping language concise and simple, saying exactly what you mean, telling the student specifically what to do, breaking down tasks into components, and teaching nonliteral language (i.e., metaphors, idioms). Table 8 overviews some examples of how to simplify language for the student with AS/HFA.

Table 8

EXAMPLES OF HOW TO SIMPLIFY LANGUAGE FOR STUDENTS WITH AS/HFA

Instead of Saying ...	Say or Do This Instead ...
"Clean up the science lab."	"Put the microscopes back on the shelf."
"Work on your project."	"Write down all the resources you will need for your social studies paper."
"Get out your literature book, turn to page 37, get out your pencil and paper."	Write the instructions on the whiteboard and call students' attention to them.
"Remember, when you go to the library, you can catch more flies with honey than vinegar."	"Remember, when you go to the library, you can catch more flies with honey than vinegar. That means you are more likely to get what you want or need if you are polite."
"Write a report on HIV by next Friday."	Write on the whiteboard and say to student: • Write a two-page report on HIV. • The report is due on Friday, March 15. • Reports should be neatly handwritten or typed. • Grammar, spelling, and organization of the report will all be counted when assigning a grade. • Examples of two reports that received an "A" and "B" are in the red folder on the health table. Also include a timeline (see Table 6).

Another helpful strategy is to provide a checklist that breaks larger tasks into more manageable parts that can be checked off when completed. This also serves as a visual support. Such organizational tools help reduce and relieve stress and anxiety.

Table 9

TIMELINE FOR HIV PROJECT

Please check items off when they are completed.

Mrs. Tyler can help you during 3rd period each day, if you wish.

Check Here	Date Due	Activity
	March 3	Have 3 resources (articles/books) downloaded or checked out.
	March 5	Outline 3 main topics about HIV you are going to write about.
	March 8	Fill in supporting sentences.
	March 10	Rewrite or type the paper, incorporating feedback from Mrs. Tyler. Check for spelling and grammar.

Teach Hidden Curriculum Rules

Given their tendency to be literal and see the world at a very literal, static level, it is no wonder that most students with AS/HFA have difficulties understanding those subtle, unwritten rules that guide and dictate social behavior in different contexts.

While most neurotypical students pick these rules up almost through osmosis, they must be taught directly to students with AS/HFA. The following examples are reprinted with permission from the book *The Hidden Curriculum: Practical Solutions for Understanding Unstated Rules in Social Situations* (Myles, Trautman, & Schelvan, 2004). A newly published Hidden Curriculum: One-A-Day Calendar (Myles, 2006) makes the task of teaching the hidden curriculum convenient and fun.

SAMPLE ITEMS FROM THE HIDDEN CURRICULUM FOR SCHOOL

- **Locker Room:** If there are people taking showers or changing their clothes, do not stare at them or make comments about their bodies.

- **Recess and P.E.:** If you are throwing a ball to someone in the gym or at recess, say her name out loud and wait until she looks and has her hands out before throwing it.

- **Lockers and the Hallway:** You may get bumped in a crowded hallway. It is usually an accident.

- **Lunchroom:** Never throw food in the lunchroom, even if other students do.

- **Assignments:** It is inappropriate to comment on other students' work quality, unless the entire class is discussing how they can improve their work.

- **Rules When Talking to the Teacher:** If you disagree with what a teacher is saying, politely say what you think and wait for an answer. If you still disagree, let it go.

- **Classroom Rules:** Limit yourself to approximately five questions during a class period. If you continue to ask questions, it may bother the other students and the teacher.

6.
SET A CALM, POSITIVE TONE

Many students with AS/HFA live with a high level of anxiety that impacts their reactions to teachers, peers, tests, changes in the environment, etc. Yet, even though they are not proficient in understanding social subtleties, individuals with AS/HFA can detect highly emotional content, such as when a fellow student panics about a test or a teacher becomes tense about constant interruptions from the school principal. In turn, they often take on the emotional tone of the person in distress by panicking or yelling.

Because individuals with AS/HFA have trouble de-stressing when they are upset, their behavior tends to escalate, often to a full-blown meltdown. Thus, it is important to set the tone in class by (a) using a calm voice when speaking; (b) giving facts in an unemotional tone of voice; (c) expressing information in a logical sequence; and (d) controlling the tendency to become intense, passionate or stressed. A calm teacher results in a calm student.

Model Acceptance

Another way to set the tone is by modeling positive acceptance. The majority of students with AS/HFA are bullied, with bullying occurring primarily in the classroom and hallways of schools. This makes it particularly important that teachers take a prominent role in preventing bullying. The way in which the teacher interacts with his student with AS/HFA sets the tone for how peers interact with the student. All students, including those with AS/HFA, perform best when they are appreciated and accepted for who they are.

SET A POSITIVE EXAMPLE

When Mr. McIlwee introduced the social studies unit on the Civil War, he told the class that Jason would be an asset to the class because of his knowledge on Civil War generals. Several students then approached Jason about working with them on their social studies project.

7. LIVE OUT LOUD

Many students with AS/HFA have difficulties with problem solving. They don't know how to systematically solve problems. *Living out loud* is strategy that facilitates problem solving and helps students understand their environment and be successful.

SATELLITE VERSUS SATELLITE

Let's suppose that Miss Hawthorne is working on a computer next to Miguel, a student with AS/HFA. Miss Hawthorne is trying to find specific information on the Internet on satellites for her science class. She begins by entering the word "satellite." Her search brings up "satellite offices." She might then say, "I need to find some information on satellites for our science class. I wonder what word I should use to begin my search. I think I'll type in 'satellite.' Oh, let's see what information came up with the search word – satellite. Ummm … I see some sites on satellite offices and satellite TV, but nothing on satellites in space. I wonder what other word I could use that might get me the kind of information I'm seeking. Maybe I can try 'space satellites'."

Verbalize Your Actions

Stating what you are doing aloud helps the student accurately put together *what* you are doing as well as the *why* and the *how*. Students with AS/HFA are often distracted by nonessential information and are unsure which details are relevant to attend to. Living out loud helps the student stay on task and understand the salient pieces in a given situation. In addition, this technique can be used to prepare the student for upcoming activities, as illustrated below.

BEING FOREWARNED

Before Ms. Chou began to circulate through the class to help her students with their independent work, she said, "I am going to walk around the classroom to see if anyone needs help so that they can get the best grades possible." Roger, who often felt a degree of anxiety because his teachers were "spying" on him, did not feel this way when Ms. Chou approached his desk because he knew *what* she was doing and *why*.

Living out loud is an excellent strategy to use to model problem solving. When the teacher misplaces a book and verbally walks herself through the last places she saw the book, the student can learn that (a) problems are generally not significant and, thus, do not require a meltdown; and (b) there is a systematic way to solve problems that includes maintaining a calm demeanor.

As mentioned earlier, *priming* is another way to live out loud. Priming is an intervention in which the student is prepared for an upcoming activity – whether for the whole day (see page 10) or for a special event – as illustrated in the following.

STEP-BY-STEP AGENDA

Mrs. Hildreth always gives precise details verbally and in written format about field trips. "At around 9:30, we will take a bus ride to the University Science Laboratory that will last approximately 20 minutes. When we arrive at the lab, we will have a brief bathroom break followed by a one-hour tour of the robotics lab. Then we will have lunch in the university cafeteria. We will have approximately 45 minutes for lunch. Then we will depart for school. We should arrive back at school at approximately 12:30."

8.
BE GENEROUS WITH PRAISE

Many students with AS/HFA have low self-esteem and limited self-confidence. As a result they are often afraid to take risks. For example, they may be hesitant to try to complete a type of assignment they have never done before or fail to initiate an interaction with peers on the playground.

Provide specific praise often so that the student can see himself as a valued individual. Find opportunities throughout the day to tell the student what he did right. Compliment his attempts — even if they fail, especially in the beginning — as well as his successes. Be specific to ensure that he knows why the praise is being provided. Simple statements can make all of the difference in the world.

USE SPECIFIC AND ONGOING PRAISE

"Good morning, Danny. I'm glad to see you."

"Kyra, I can always count on you to pick an interesting topic for your papers!"

"Maria, show Mr. Smith the terrific science project you did."

"I noticed you held the door open for Mr. Hake when he had his hands full, Taku. That was so thoughtful."

Foster Attribution and Understanding

Praise also teaches attribution or an understanding of why things happen. Children with AS/HFA often do not know why things occur and, therefore, make incorrect attributions about events. For example, a student may not know that the reason she did well on a test was because she studied. She is more likely to attribute success to "being lucky" or the test being easy. Students with AS/HFA generally do not understand that their effort can impact results. A simple statement, such as "You did well on your history test. Your studying really paid off," can begin to help a student understand that his effort contributed to his grade.

MAKE STUDENTS SEE THE RESULTS OF THEIR EFFORTS

Ms. Mehaffey and Bill had spent the last five minutes of each day going over his planner to ensure that all assignments were listed along with their due dates. At the end of the second week of this process, Ms. Mehaffey remarked to Bill that since they had started reviewing his planner, all his assignments had been turned in on time and he was getting an "A" in math. This helped Bill to see the tangible results of having an accurate planner.

9.
LISTEN TO THE WORDS

The manner in which a student with AS/HFA conveys a message may not indicate its significance. Often these students use a monotone voice with little facial expression to discuss an item of importance or even urgency. To detect the true meaning of a message, listen to the student, interpret what she is saying literally, and probe.

LISTEN AND PROBE

When Kaitlin said quietly to her teacher, "I don't want to ride the bus home," Ms. King was tempted to say, "It's only a 15-minute ride, so what's the big deal?" But instead, she asked Kaitlin to tell her about the bus ride. After carefully listening to Kaitlin and asking several probing questions, Ms. King was able to interpret her concern. Although her voice tone did not convey her emotions, Kaitlin was very upset about riding the bus. During the past week, Kaitlin had had her lunch taken from her twice, been pinched frequently, and had been forced to relinquish two of her treasured Hello Kitty™ keychains. The older girl who had bullied her had threatened her if she told. It was only through Ms. King's gentle persistence that Kaitlin revealed why she did not want to ride the bus.

Seek and Offer Clarification

Encourage the student to clarify what he means. If a student says, "I can't do this," probe further. Ask him what he means. This statement could have many meanings, including:

1. I can't find my book.
2. I don't understand the directions.
3. I have to go to the bathroom *now* and can't do my assignment until after I go.
4. I can't concentrate because I am upset that I lost my Pokémon™ card.
5. I need help with the first problem.
6. My pencil lead broke and the rule is that we can only sharpen pencils between classes.

10.
PROVIDE REASSURANCE

Students with AS/HFA become anxious if they do not feel they know what to do. To make matters worse, they tend not to ask questions when uncertain, making it difficult to know that they don't understand what they are supposed to do. Further, these students often cannot accurately anticipate a logical time frame or sequence of events and, therefore, are unsure about what they are to do.

Reduce Uncertainty

Uncertainty creates anxiety that, in turn, reduces students' ability to attend and learn while increasing the risk of tantrums, rage, and meltdowns.

NEGATIVE EFFECTS OF UNCERTAINTY

Jada, a high school student with AS/HFA, had set up a meeting with a career counselor at her local community college to discuss her vocational interests and courses that she might take when she finished high school. The counselor agreed to meet Jada on a Saturday at 9:00 a.m.

Jada prepared carefully for the meeting, working with her parents to develop a list of questions to ask and dressing in a way that would communicate that she would be a serious student. The counselor neglected to indicate how long the meeting would last so, unbeknownst to her parents, Jada packed a lunch and dinner to take to the meeting. She was mortified when she appeared at the meeting with the two meals, only to be told that the meeting would last approximately one hour. During the meeting Jada barely heard what the counselor was saying and did not ask her carefully planned questions because she was so upset about her social faux pas.

Students with AS/HFA need reassurance about upcoming events. The following simple strategies can help students feel more confident and composed. Often these strategies overlap and are used in combination to provide the most supportive environment.

Table 10

STRATEGIES TO HELP STUDENTS FEEL CONFIDENT AND COMPOSED

- Provide a daily schedule and refer to it frequently. For example, at the end of math class, tell the student and the class that math is ending and that reading will begin in 5 minutes.

- Instead of a traditional clock, use a time timer (timetimer.com) or other visual timer in class. This will allow students to see the passage of time.

- Teach nonliteral language associated with time. For example, let the student know that expressions such as "just a second" or "in a minute" do not refer to exact time segments. Rather, they indicate that assistance will be forthcoming, but will not be immediate. "Wait a minute" does not mean stopping and counting to 60; it means waiting a short period of time until told otherwise.

- Break tasks into segments and communicate how long each task is expected to take.

BREAK DOWN THE TASK INTO SMALLER STEPS AND PROVIDE ONGOING FEEDBACK

When Mr. Bueller told his students to write three paragraphs about the current event they had brought to class, he told them they had 30 minutes to complete the task. He suggested that they spend approximately 5 minutes thinking about the structure, 5 minutes outlining the brief paper, and 10 minutes working on each section. In addition, he handed each student a checklist showing the steps, and while circulating around the room, he quietly announced the time of each designated sequence. Chris, a student with AS/HFA, typed his assignment following Mr. Bueller's timeline. Mr. Bueller checked on Chris frequently, letting him know that he was progressing as expected on the assignment and offering other feedback as appropriate.

Providing reassurance also helps students maintain appropriate behavior. Utilizing "check-ins" by making frequent contact helps the student with AS/HFA know that (a) his behavior is appropriate and (b) his progress on assignments is suitable. This reduces anxiety and promotes on-task behavior.

CHECK IN ON A REGULAR BASIS AND PROVIDE REASSURANCE

Keenon's paraprofessional, Ms. Otto, used frequent check-ins with him and other students throughout the day. She tried to be specific. "Keenon, I like the way you are working on your book report. I'm going to hand in the attendance sheets to Mr. Smith and I'll be back shortly. Keep up the good work."

In addition to providing reassurance, check-ins are also reinforcing. Commenting to the student "I like the way you are _____" provides valuable information by telling the student that he is doing what is expected. Marv, a student with AS/HFA, and Terry did not get along in class. When they were in sitting in close proximity, they often ended up in arguments. Nevertheless, Marv elected to be in groups with Terry, and inevitably they ended up arguing. One day when Marv selected to partner with another student, his teacher quietly said to him, "I like the way you decided to partner with Patrick on this project. He and you work together well without arguing."

Provide information and reassurance frequently so that the student knows he is moving in the right direction, engaging in appropriate behavior, or completing the correct task. Frequent check-ins are an easy way to monitor student progress and stress.

Summary

Students with AS/HFA live in a world that is often puzzling and unpredictable to them and, therefore, stressful. In order to help them meet their potential, educators must help these students understand the world around them and provide them with strategies and supports that will foster success and independence.

The 10 helpful hints presented here offer easy-to-use strategies and considerations that can be implemented across educational settings. Best of all, they require little teacher time, but their impact is tremendous! These strategies can make the difference between a successful and unsuccessful school experience for an otherwise talented and able student.

REFERENCES

Buron, K. D. (2006). *When my worries gets too big! A relaxation book for children who live with anxiety.* Shawnee Mission, KS: Autism Asperger Publishing Company.

Buron, K. D., & Curtis, M. (2003). *The incredible 5-point scale: Assisting students with autism spectrum disorders in understanding social interactions and controlling their emotional responses.* Shawnee Mission, KS: Autism Asperger Publishing Company.

Buron, K. D., & Curtis, M. (2003). *The incredible 5-point scale: Assisting students with autism spectrum disorders in understanding social interactions and controlling their emotional responses.* [DVD] Shawnee Mission, KS: Autism Asperger Publishing Company.

Cardon, T. A. (2004). *Let's talk emotions: Helping children with social cognitive deficits, including AS, HFA, and NVLD, learn to understand and express empathy and emotions.* Shawnee Mission, KS: Autism Asperger Publishing Company.

Coucouvanis, J. (2005). *Super skills: A social skills group program for children with Asperger Syndrome, high-functioning autism and related challenges.* Shawnee Mission, KS: Autism Asperger Publishing Company.

Gagnon, E. (2001). *Power Cards: Using special interests to motivate children and youth with Asperger Syndrome and autism.* Shawnee Mission, KS: Autism Asperger Publishing Company.

Gray, C. (2000). *The new Social Story™ book: Illustrated edition.* Arlington, TX: Future Horizons.

Heinrichs, R. (2003). *Perfect targets – Asperger Syndrome and bullying: Practical solutions for surviving the social world.* Shawnee Mission, KS: Autism Asperger Publishing Company.

Moore, S. T. (2002). *Asperger Syndrome and the elementary school experience: Practical solutions for academic and social difficulties.* Shawnee Mission, KS: Autism Asperger Publishing Company.

Myles, B. S. (2005). *The hidden curriculum: Teaching what is meaningful.* [DVD]

Myles, B. S. (2005). *The hidden curriculum: Teaching what is meaningful.* [DVD] Shawnee Mission, KS: Autism Asperger Publishing Company.

Myles, B. S. (2006). *Hidden curriculum: One-a-day calendar. Practical solutions for understanding unstated rules in social situations.* Shawnee Mission, KS; Autism Asperger Publishing Company.

Myles, B.S., Trautman, M.L., & Schelvan, R.L. (2004). *The hidden curriculum: Practical solutions for understanding unstated rules in social situations.* Shawnee Mission, KS; Autism Asperger Publishing Company.

Myles, B. S., & Adreon, D. (2001). *Asperger Syndrome and adolescence: Practical solutions for school success.* Shawnee Mission, KS: Autism Asperger Publishing Company.

Myles, B. S., Adreon, D. A., Hagen, K., Holverstott, J., Hubbard, A., Smith, S. M., & Trautman, M. (2005). *Life journey through autism: An educator's guide to Asperger Syndrome.* Arlington, VA: Organization for Autism Research.

Myles, B. S., Cook, K. T., Miller, N. E., Rinner, L., & Robbins, L. (2000). *Asperger Syndrome and sensory issues: Practical solutions for making sense of the world.* Shawnee Mission, KS: Autism Asperger Publishing Company.

Myles, B. S., & Southwick, J. (2005). *Asperger Syndrome and difficult moments: Practical solutions for tantrums, rage, and meltdowns (2nd ed.).* Shawnee Mission, KS: Autism Asperger Publishing Company.

Myles, H. M. (2002). *Practical solutions to everyday challenges for children with Asperger Syndrome.* Shawnee Mission, KS: Autism Asperger Publishing Company.

Sakai, K. (2005). *Finding our way: Practical solutions for creating a supportive home and community for the Asperger Syndrome family.* Shawnee Mission, KS: Autism Asperger Publishing Company.

Printed in the USA
CPSIA information can be obtained
at www.ICGtesting.com
JSHW061135261023
50925JS00002B/4